My name is

_____.

Will you please read to me?
Thank you.

ZONDERKIDZ

The Beginner's Bible® Carry-Along Treasury
Copyright © 2005 by Zondervan
Illustrations © 2005, 2016 by Zondervan

Requests for information should be addressed to:
Zondervan, 3900 Sparks Dr. SE, Grand Rapids, Michigan 49546

ISBN 978-0-310-76030-6

Illustrations: Denis Alonso
Art Direction and Design: Jody Langley

Printed in China

23 24 25 26 27 /LPC/ 17 16 15 14 13 12 11 10 9 8 7 6 5

The Beginner's Bible® Carry-Along Treasury

ZONDERkidz

Contents

OLD TESTAMENT

NEW TESTAMENT

The Old Testament

The Beginning

Genesis 1

In the beginning, the world was empty.
Darkness was everywhere.
But God had a plan.

God separated the light from the darkness.
"Let there be light!" he said.
And the light turned on.
He called the light "day."
And he called the darkness "night."
This was the end of the very first day.

Then God said, "I will divide the waters."
He separated the waters in the clouds
above from the waters in the ocean below.
He called the space between them "sky."
This was the end of the second day.

Next, God rolled back the waters
and some dry ground appeared.
He made plants of many shapes and colors.
He made mountains, hills, and valleys.
This was the end of the third day.

God put a shining sun in
the sky for daytime.
He put a glowing moon and twinkling
stars in the sky for nighttime.
This was the end of the fourth day.

On the fifth day,
God made swishy fish and
squiggly creatures to live in the ocean.
Then God made birds
to fly across the sky.

On the sixth day, God made animals
to creep, crawl, hop, and gallop.
Then from the dust, God made the most
wonderful creature of all—a person.
God named him Adam.
On the seventh day, God rested.

Adam and Eve

Genesis 2

God had planted a beautiful garden for
Adam in a place called Eden.
A river flowed through the garden.

Adam loved his new home.
His job was to name all the animals
and care for the garden.
Adam loved all the animals,
but he could not find a friend
that was just right for him.
So God created a woman.

Adam named her Eve.
She was just right for Adam.
Adam and Eve loved each other.
Together they took care
of God's garden.

The Sneaky Snake

Genesis 3

Many trees grew in the Garden of Eden.
God told Adam and Eve, "You may eat
the fruit from any tree except for one.
Never eat the fruit from the Tree
of the Knowledge of Good and Evil."

Now, there was a sneaky snake
in the garden.
One day, the snake saw Eve
near the special tree.
It hissed, "Did God *really* tell you
not to eat the fruit from this tree?"

The snake wanted Eve to disobey God.
It said, "You should try some
of this tasty fruit.
If you eat it, you will be like God.
You will be able to tell the difference
between good and evil."

The fruit looked tasty.
Eve remembered what God had said,
but she ate the fruit anyway.
Then Eve gave some to Adam.
He took a bite too.

As the sun was going down,
Adam and Eve heard God
walking through the garden.
He was looking for them.
Adam and Eve hid among the trees.
They were afraid.

"What have you done?" God asked.
"Did you eat the fruit from
the forbidden tree?"
Adam said, "Yes, but Eve gave it to me."
Eve said, "Yes, but the snake tricked me."

God told the snake, "Because of what you
did, you will always crawl on your belly."
Then he told Adam and Eve,
"Because you disobeyed me,
you can no longer live in the garden."

Adam and Eve left the garden.
God placed angels and a flaming sword
to guard the entrance.
Adam and Eve would not be allowed
in the garden again.

Noah's Ark

Genesis 6–9

After Adam and Eve left the garden,
many people were born.
The people kept doing bad things,
and they forgot about God.

Except Noah. Noah loved God.

God was sad that everyone but Noah
forgot about him.
He told Noah about his plan to start over.
"Make yourself an ark," God said.
"Here's how." So Noah and his family
began working on the ark.

When it was done, God said,
"Take your family and two of
every animal into the ark."
Animals creeped, crawled, hopped,
and galloped onto Noah's new boat.

After everyone was inside,
the rain began to fall.
And fall. And fall.
The ark rocked this way and
that way on the rising water.

Finally, the rain stopped.
Water covered everything!
Everyone inside the ark was safe.
Noah and his family were very happy.

One day, Noah sent a dove to find land.
It flew and flew but never found any.
So it came back. One week later,
Noah sent the dove out again.
This time it brought him an olive leaf.
Noah cheered, "It must have found land!"

The ark finally came to rest on
the top of a mountain.
God told Noah to leave the ark.
Noah and his family praised God.
God put a beautiful rainbow in the sky.
It was a sign of his promise to
never flood the whole earth again.

A Baby in a Basket

Exodus 1–2:10

God's people were living in Egypt. They were called Israelites. The ruler in Egypt was called Pharaoh and he did not like God's people.

Pharaoh made them work hard. They were slaves. One day, Pharaoh decided to get rid of all the Israelite baby boys.

A woman named Jochebed had a baby
boy. She wanted to save him.
So she gently laid her baby inside a basket
and placed him in the river.
The baby started to cry.

Pharaoh's daughter saw the basket
and opened it.
She gently picked up the baby and
hugged him. "I want to keep you,"
the princess whispered.
She named him Moses because
she pulled him out of the water.

Miriam, the baby's big sister,
had been watching nearby.
She said to the princess, "I know a woman
who can help you take care of the baby."
So Miriam ran to get her mother.
Jochebed was so happy!

When Moses was a young boy,
Jochebed returned him to the princess.
He grew up in the palace.

The Burning Bush

Exodus 3

When Moses was a man,
he left the palace.
Pharaoh was still being mean
to the Israelites.
Moses tried to protect them,
so Pharaoh tried to kill Moses.

Moses escaped from Egypt.
He went to a place called Midian
and became a shepherd.

One day, while Moses was watching
his sheep, he saw something strange.
A bush was on fire, but it wasn't
burning up. From inside the bush,
God spoke, "Moses, bring my
people out of Egypt. Take them
to a new land that I will show you.
This new land is called Canaan."

Moses was worried that Pharaoh
would not listen. God told Moses
to throw his staff on the ground.
When he did, the staff became a snake!
God told Moses to reach down and grab
the snake. It became a staff again!
God said, "I will use signs like this
to show Pharaoh I have sent you."

"But I cannot speak very well,"
complained Moses.
God said, "Do not worry.
Your brother Aaron is a good speaker.
I will send him with you."

So Moses returned with Aaron to Egypt.
When they arrived, Moses told the
Israelites what God had said.

Ten Plagues

Exodus 7–12

Moses and Aaron went to
Pharaoh's palace. They said,
"You must let the Israelites go free.
If you do not, God will punish you."

Pharaoh said, "No! I do not
know your God!"
Then he made the Israelites
work even harder.

God was not pleased.
So he changed the main river to blood.
Pharaoh did not care. "I will never
let the Israelites go," he said.

Then God sent frogs to Egypt.
They were sitting in chairs, hopping up
stairs, and jumping all over the beds.
Pharaoh said, "Take the frogs away, and
I will let your people go."
So God took the frogs away.

But Pharaoh changed his mind
and said, "No."
God sent more plagues on Egypt.
First were the pesky gnats.
Then came a frenzy of flies.
Next, all the animals got sick.
Then the Egyptians' skin broke
out in sores.

Damaging hailstorms came,
and then swarms of locusts ate the crops.
Then darkness covered everything.
Sometimes Pharaoh said he would
let the people go.
But after God took away each plague,
Pharaoh changed his mind and said, "No."

Moses had one last message from God
for Pharaoh: "If you do not let my
people go, the firstborn son in each
Egyptian family will die."
Pharaoh refused to listen.
So God kept his promise.
Pharaoh finally said, "Go now!"

The Red Sea

Exodus 14

Moses led the Israelites out of Egypt.
During the day, God went ahead of them
in a pillar of cloud. During the night,
God went ahead of them in a pillar of fire.

God led the Israelites to the
edge of the Red Sea.
Pharaoh and his army were close behind.
The Israelites did not know what to do.

They screamed, "We are trapped!
What have you done to us, Moses?"
Moses said, "Do not be afraid.
God will protect us." God's cloud came
between the Israelites and Pharaoh's army.
They could not see anything!

God told Moses, "Raise your staff
over the sea." Then the Lord pushed
back the sea to make a path.
Moses and the Israelites followed the path
through the sea and to the other side.
But Pharaoh's army followed close behind.

Moses raised his staff again, and
the sea swept away Pharaoh and his army.
Moses and all the Israelites sang praises
to God. They were free!
They weren't slaves anymore!

Deborah Leads the Way

Judges 4

The Israelites lived in the
promised land for many years.
But they forgot about God.
A bad king from another land
ruled over them.
The Israelites asked God for help.

God sent them a judge named Deborah.
She loved God very much.
God gave her a plan to defeat the bad
king. She sent for a man named Barak
and told him, "God wants you to take
10,000 soldiers and wait on the hill."

The Israelites were not as
strong as their enemies.
Barak begged Deborah to go with them.
She was a strong leader. She agreed.

When the Israelites met face to face
with the king's army, Deborah exclaimed,
"Go! Attack them now! God is with us!"
The Israelites obeyed and won the battle.

Samson

Judges 13; 16

The Israelites were in trouble again.
Along came a very strong man
named Samson. God had chosen
him to save the Israelites from
their enemies, the Philistines.

Samson knew that as long as
he did not cut his hair,
he would always be very strong.

Samson was in love with Delilah.
The Philistines told Delilah they
would pay her if she found out
what made Samson so strong.
At first, Samson lied to her.

"If you tie me up with ropes,"
Samson said, "I will lose my strength."
That night while Samson slept,
Delilah tied him up. Then she shouted,
"The Philistines are coming!"
Samson jumped up and broke the ropes.
Delilah kissed him and asked,
"Won't you tell me your secret?"

Samson gave in and told her,
"My strength is in my long hair."
When Samson was asleep,
Delilah had all his hair cut off.
Samson's strength was gone!
The Philistines grabbed him
and put him in jail.

A while later, the Philistines were having
a big party. They brought Samson in
and made fun of him.
Samson prayed to God to make him
strong one last time. God did.
Samson pushed the pillars with all his might.
The temple came crashing down, and
Samson defeated the Philistines.

Ruth and Naomi

Ruth 1–4

Naomi grew up in the promised land,
which was also called Israel.
But now she lived far away.
She had a husband and two sons.
Ruth was married to one of the sons.
Then something sad happened.
Naomi's husband and sons died.
Not long after that, Naomi decided
to go back to her homeland.

Naomi told Ruth to return to her parents, but
Ruth did not want to leave her.
She loved Naomi so much.
"I will go wherever you go," Ruth said.
"Your home will be my home.
Your God will be my God."
So Ruth went with Naomi to Israel.

They needed food to eat. So each day,
Ruth gathered leftover grain from the
fields. A good man named Boaz owned
the land. One day, he saw Ruth in the
field. He wanted to help her. So he
left extra grain for Ruth to gather.

Boaz fell in love with Ruth. They got
married and had a baby boy named Obed.
God had blessed Ruth and Grandma Naomi
with a brand-new family.

David and Goliath

1 Samuel 17:1–51

The Philistines were enemies of God.
Their army came to fight King Saul's army.
A giant soldier named Goliath yelled, "Bring
out your best soldier to fight me!"

"If your strongest soldier defeats me,
we will be your slaves!" he boomed.
"If I defeat him, you will be our slaves!"
King Saul's soldiers were afraid.
They did not want to fight the giant.

Meanwhile, a young boy named David
was taking food to his brothers. They
were soldiers in King Saul's army.
When David reached the camp,
he heard the giant's challenge.

"I am not afraid to fight the giant,"
said David. King Saul called for
David and told him, "You cannot fight
the giant. You are too young."
David replied, "God will be with me."

King Saul gave his armor to David,
but it was big and heavy.
David wasn't used to wearing armor.

David went to a nearby stream
and picked up five stones.
He stood before Goliath.
The giant laughed at him, but
David didn't care. He said,
"I come before you in the name
of the LORD who rules over all."

David put a stone in his sling
and ran toward the giant.
Then he let the stone fly.

It hit Goliath's forehead,
and he fell to the ground!
The Philistines saw that their hero
was dead. They ran away.

The Brave Queen

Esther 1–10

Esther was Jewish. That means she was
an Israelite. She lived in the land of Persia
with her older cousin Mordecai.

The king of Persia needed a new queen.
He announced, "Bring me the most
beautiful women from all over my
kingdom." Esther was one of the women
sent to the palace. When the king met
Esther, he chose her to be his queen.

Haman was the king's chief helper.
He hated the Jewish people. They were
God's people. Haman wanted everyone
to bow down to him. Mordecai refused
to bow down to Haman. Mordecai would
only bow down to God.

Haman went to the king. He said,
"The Jews are bad people. You should sign a
law that will help me get rid of them."
So the king signed the new law.
God's people were in great danger!

Mordecai heard about the new law.
He ran to tell Esther, "You must save
yourself and the rest of God's people.
Perhaps God has made you the
queen for this reason."
So Esther came up with a plan.
It would be very risky for her.

Esther invited the king and Haman to
a special dinner. Then she asked the king,
"Why does Haman want to get rid of me?"
The king was surprised. She said,
"I am Jewish. Haman tricked you into
signing a new law that would get rid
of all the Jews."

The king told his guards, "Arrest Haman!"
Then he made Mordecai his new
chief helper. He told Queen Esther,
"I will make a new law that will keep
you and your people safe."
God used Esther to save his people!

Daniel and the Lions

Daniel 6

Darius became the new king of Babylon.
Daniel was his chief helper. The king's
other helpers did not like Daniel.

They said to the king, "You are such a wonderful king. You should make a new law that for the next 30 days, everyone must pray only to you. If they disobey, they will be thrown into the lions' den."

King Darius made the new law, but
Daniel kept praying to God because
Daniel loved God. The king's helpers
caught him praying.

They told King Darius, "Now you must
throw Daniel into the lions' den."
The king knew he had been tricked,
but he had to obey his new law.

Daniel was thrown into the lions' den.
He was not afraid. He knew God would
take care of him. King Darius told Daniel,
"I hope your God will save you."
That night, the king could not sleep.
He was too worried about Daniel.

At sunrise, the king hurried to the lions' den.
"Has your God saved you from the lions?" he
called. "Yes!" answered Daniel.
"My God sent his angel to protect me."
So Daniel returned to the palace. Then
King Darius ordered everyone to honor and
respect God.

Jonah and the Big Fish

Jonah 1:1–3:10

Jonah was a prophet of God.
One day, God told Jonah,
"Go to the big city of Nineveh.
Tell them to stop doing bad things."

But Jonah ran away. He did not want
to go to Nineveh. Instead he got on
a boat to sail across the sea.
God sent a big storm to stop Jonah.
The sailors on the boat were afraid.
They thought the boat was going to sink!

Jonah told the sailors,
"My God has sent this storm.
If you throw me into the water,
the sea will become calm again."

So the sailors threw Jonah
into the raging sea.
Instantly, the sea became calm.

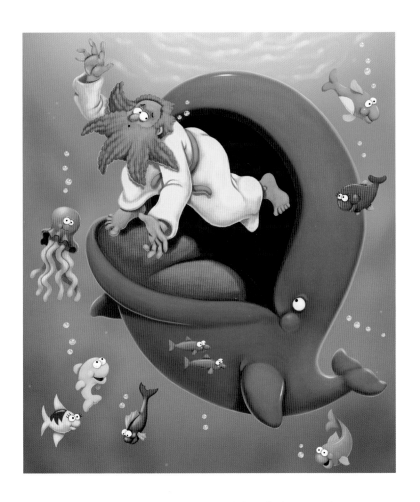

Just then, Jonah saw a big fish coming!
Gulp! The fish swallowed Jonah.

For three days and nights, Jonah was
inside the fish. He prayed to God,
"Please forgive me."

Then God told the fish to spit Jonah onto dry
land. God told Jonah a second time,
"Go and tell the people of Nineveh
to stop doing bad things."

This time, Jonah obeyed God.
The people in Nineveh
were sorry for doing bad things,
so God forgave them.

The New Testament

Baby Jesus Is Born

Luke 2:1–7

Mary loved Joseph. Mary and Joseph were going to be married soon.
Joseph lived in Nazareth, but his family came from Bethlehem.

A new leader named Caesar ordered all
people to go back to their homeland.
He wanted to count all the people
in his kingdom. So Mary and Joseph
went to Bethlehem.

Mary was going to have her baby soon.
When they arrived in Bethlehem,
they looked for a safe place to sleep,
but all the inns were full.

Finally, a man was able to help them.
He said, "I do not have any rooms left,
but you are welcome to sleep
in the stable."

Joseph made a warm place for Mary
to rest. While they were there,
little baby Jesus was born.

Mary wrapped Jesus in strips of cloth
and gently laid him in a manger.

Jesus Chooses His Disciples

Matthew 4:18–22; 9:9; 10:1–4; Mark 1–3; Luke 5–6

Jesus began to tell people about God.
He knew he had a lot of work to do,
and he went to find some helpers.

As Jesus was walking along the seashore,
he saw some fishermen.
Jesus called to them, "Come. Follow me.
I will make you fishers of people."

Right away, they left their boats
and followed Jesus. Their names were
Peter, Andrew, James, and John.

Later, Jesus met a tax collector named
Matthew. His job was to get the tax money
from the people and give it to the king.
Matthew quit his job to follow Jesus too.

Jesus chose some more people.
Their names were Philip, Bartholomew,
Thomas, and another man named James.

JOHN
JAMES SON OF ZEBEDEE
PETER
MATTHEW
ANDREW

Thaddaeus, Simon, and Judas joined them
too. Jesus now had twelve new followers.
He called them his *disciples*.
Jesus taught them about God's love.

Jesus Teaches on a Mountain

Matthew 5:1–12; 6:25–34; Luke 6:17–23; 12:22–31

All sorts of people went to see Jesus.
Children, mothers, fathers,
grandmas, and grandpas.
They all wanted to hear what
he was teaching.

"Look at the birds," said Jesus.
"Do they store up food in a barn?
No. God feeds them."

"Look at the flowers," said Jesus.
"They don't work or make clothes.
God dresses them in lush leaves
and pretty petals."

Then Jesus said, "You are much more
important than birds. You are much
more important than flowers.
So do not worry. If God takes care
of them, God will take care of you."

Jesus Calms the Storm

Matthew 8:23–27

Jesus and his disciples got into a boat.
They wanted to cross the sea.

Jesus took a nap.
The waves gently rocked
the boat back and forth.

Suddenly a great storm came up.
Waves splashed over the boat.
Winds whipped around the disciples.

They woke Jesus up and shouted,
"The boat is sinking! Don't you care?"

Jesus asked, "Why are you so afraid?
Don't you have any faith at all?"
Then Jesus told the storm to stop.
Right away it was calm.

The disciples were amazed. They said
to each other, "Who is this man Jesus?
Even the wind and the waves obey him!"

Jesus and the Children

Matthew 19:13–15; Mark 10:13–16; Luke 18:15–17

The children loved to spend time
with Jesus.

But the disciples didn't understand.
They said, "Stop. Do not bother Jesus.
He is just too busy."

Jesus told the disciples, "Let the children come to me. Do not keep them away. You must become like these little children if you want to enter God's kingdom."

Then Jesus blessed the children.

The True King

Matthew 21:1–11; Mark 11:1–11; Luke 19:29–42; John 12:12–19

Jesus and his disciples went to Jerusalem
for the Passover Feast. Jesus told
two disciples to bring him a donkey.
He told them where to find it.

Jesus rode the donkey to Jerusalem.

A big crowd welcomed him.

People waved palm branches and put them on the road in front of Jesus.

They shouted, "Hosanna! Hosanna!
Blessed is the king of Israel!"

Some of the leaders in Jerusalem did not like Jesus. They saw how people were following him, and they were angry about it. They were jealous.

The Last Supper

Matthew 26:17–29; Mark 14:12–25; Luke 22:7–19; John 13–14

Jesus was having supper with his friends.
He picked up a loaf of bread and blessed it.
Then he broke it into pieces.
He gave the bread to his disciples to eat.
Jesus said, "This bread is my body.
Every time you do this, think of me."

In the same way, he took a cup of wine
and blessed it. He gave it to the disciples
to drink. "This is my blood. It is poured
out to forgive the sins of many."

"The time has come for me to go away.
Where I am going, you cannot go yet.
I am going to heaven to prepare a
wonderful new home for you.
But I will return to you soon."

"At first, you will be very sad.
But do not be frightened.
Soon you will understand
and you will be filled with joy."

Jesus Is Arrested
and Crucified

Matthew 26–27; Mark 14–15; Luke 22–23; John 18–19

Judas went to the leaders. He asked,
"How much will you pay me if I help
you capture Jesus?" They said,
"Thirty pieces of silver." So Judas took
the money and made a plan.

Jesus had gone to his favorite garden
to pray. The disciples went along.
Jesus prayed, "Father, if it is your will,
I am ready to give my life so that
all the people who trust in me will be
saved from their sins."

Soon, Judas arrived with some soldiers.
Peter wanted to protect Jesus.
But Jesus said, "No. I must allow this
to happen." All the disciples ran away,
and the soldiers arrested Jesus.

They took Jesus to the leaders.
The leaders said, "You say that
you are the Son of God.
We do not believe you."

The soldiers took charge of Jesus.
They made him carry a big wooden cross.
They took him to a place called
The Skull (*Golgotha*).
There they nailed Jesus to the cross.

Jesus died on the cross.

Everyone who loved Jesus was very sad.
But they forgot something important. Jesus
had said he would see them again soon!

Jesus Is Risen!

Matthew 28:1–10; Mark 16:1–10; Luke 24:1–11; John 20:1–18

After Jesus died, some of his
friends laid his body in a big tomb.
They sealed it shut with a large round
stone. Soldiers guarded the tomb.

Three days later, the earth shook. An angel
of the Lord came down from heaven and
pushed the stone away from the tomb.
Then the angel sat on the stone.

When the soldiers saw the angel,
they fell to the ground.

Mary was walking to the tomb with some of her friends. They saw the angel, who said, "Do not be afraid. Jesus is not here. He has risen!"

"Go and tell Peter and the other disciples
that Jesus is alive!"

On their way, the women saw Jesus.
They fell to their knees and worshiped
him. Jesus smiled and said, "Go tell the
others that I will see them in Galilee."
So Mary ran to tell the disciples.

Jesus Goes to Heaven

Matthew 28:16–20, Luke 24:44–51; Acts 1:6–11

Jesus had told his disciples, "I gave my life
so that you could be with me in heaven.
I am going there to prepare a wonderful new
home for you. When I come back the next
time, I will take you with me."
But now it was time for Jesus to leave.

Jesus said, "God has given me
complete power over heaven and earth.
Go and tell everyone the good news.
Make new disciples. Baptize them and
teach them to obey my commandments.
Don't ever forget, I will always be
with you."

"Go to Jerusalem and wait there,"
said Jesus. "The Holy Spirit will come to
you. He will give you power to tell people
about me. Now the time has come for me
to go to heaven. Do not be afraid."

Then Jesus went up toward heaven
in a cloud. His disciples stared at the
sky for a long time.

Jesus Is Coming!

Revelation 1:1–2; 21:2–4

Many years later, the disciple John
lived on an island. While he was there,
an angel came to him in a vision.

In the vision, a bright light surrounded
Jesus. He spoke to John, "Do not be
afraid. Write a book about what you
see and send it to the churches."

In the vision, John saw God sitting on his throne. A rainbow sparkled all around him. John saw that everything bad on the earth had come to an end.

Then John saw a new heaven and a
new earth. God said, "There will be
no more death or sadness or crying or
pain. I will live with my people forever."

Then Jesus promised,
"I am coming back soon."